All Aboard!

A TRAVELING ALPHABET by BILL MAYER

concept by Chris L. Demarest

Margaret K. McElderry Books

New York   London   Toronto   Sydney

foreword

Some of my earliest memories are of traveling. I remember my dad would put my brother Bob and me on the train to visit Mammaw in Birmingham. We had a blast running up and down the train and in between the cars, and hanging out the back of the train watching the world go by.

When Ann Bobco sent this book idea to me, it didn't take long for me to get on board. Since art school, I have always loved the poster artists of the 1920s. Their bold graphic images evoked the time period and a sense of mystery about travel. My wife, Lee, and I have collected these posters over the years until we have run out of wall space.

It was a bit of a challenge to work the letter of the alphabet into the design of each image. Working with Ann and creating these images was exciting, as was seeing her playful treatment with the type. I think what we ended up with is a creative and fun homage to those early advertising artists from the twenties.   —Bill Mayer

Travel and transportation have always fascinated me. As a child, going to the airport to see my father off on business trips, I marveled at tho large, shiny planes sparkling in the sunlight, thundering down the runways, lifting off, and heading in all directions.

Transportation in the era before and after World War II was (for me) at its most interesting in terms of design. From the Ford Tri-Motor airplane to the sleek Pan Am Constellation, from the powerful black steam locomotives to the streamlined Zephyr and the stately oceanliners that ferried passengers all around the world, artists captured not only the destinations, but the mode of travel as well. How one traveled was as important as the destination.

The travel poster from those times was an art form. In bold and subtle color or black and white, the artist beckoned the yearning traveler to hop on a plane or train or bus and seek exotic destinations. This alphabet book seeks to recreate those magical times.   —Chris L. Demarest

ELEPHANT

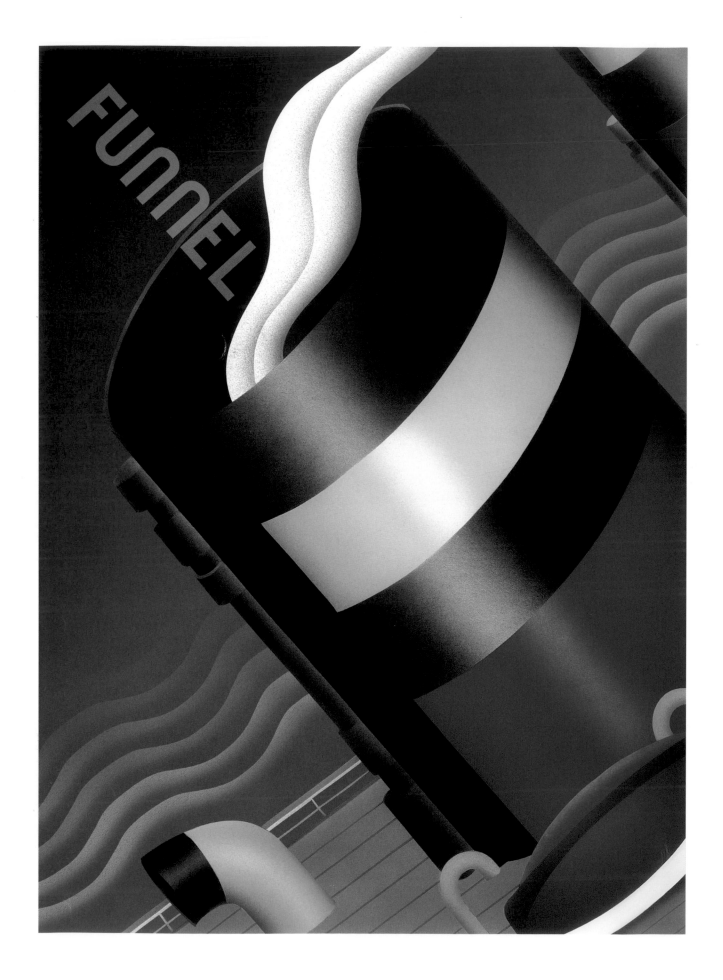

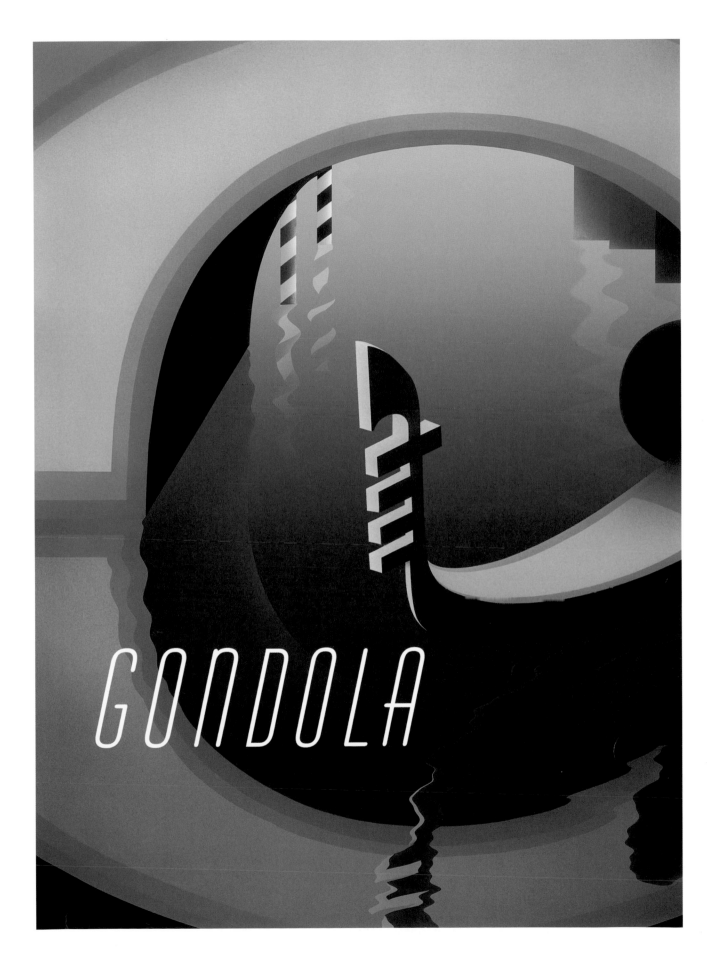

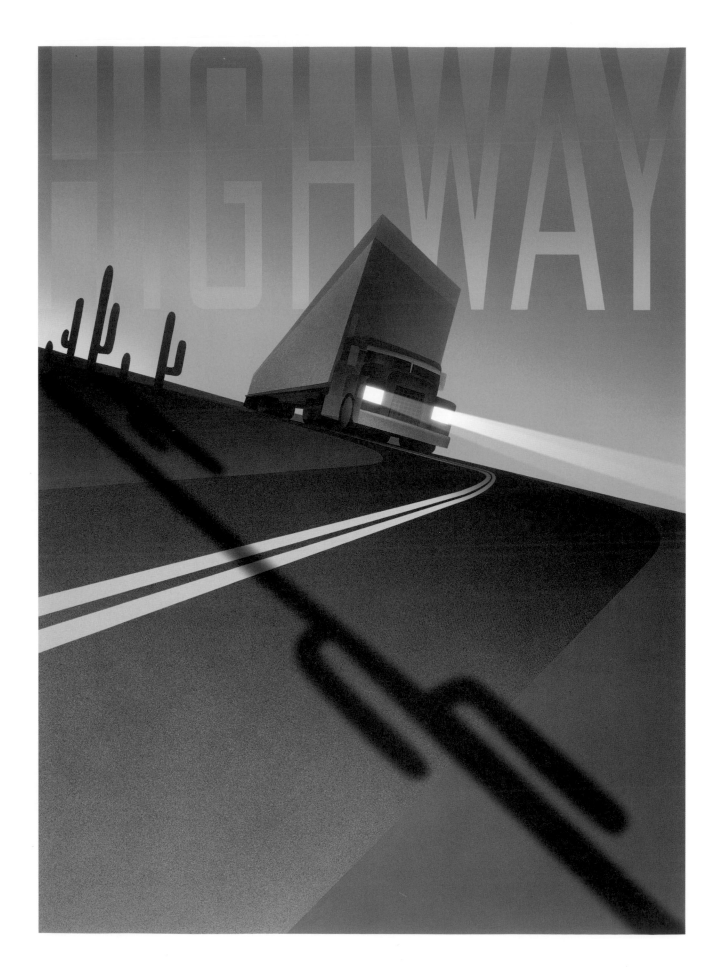

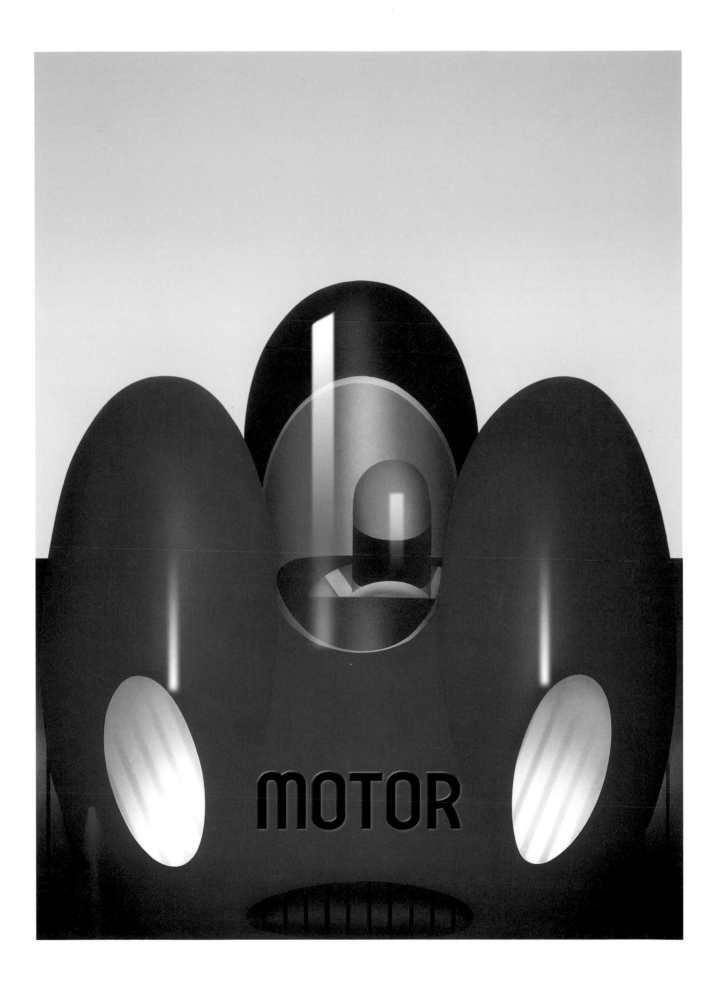

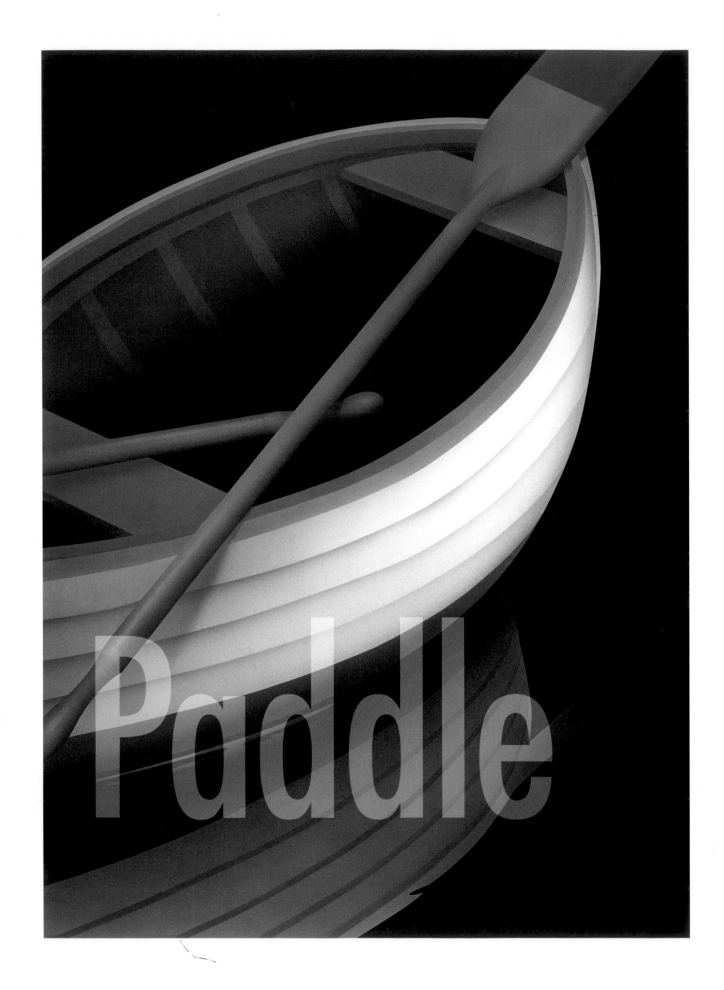

Swoosh

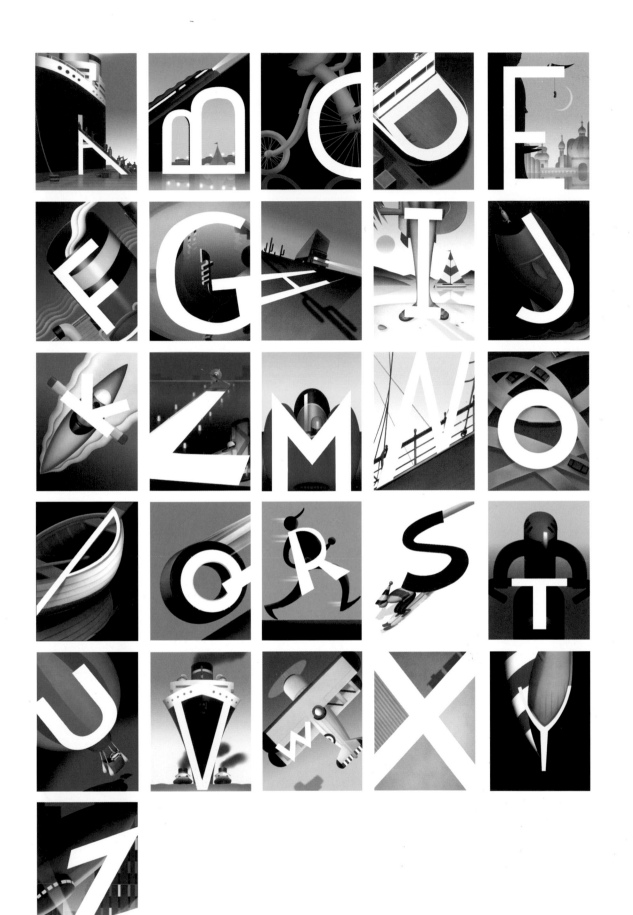

For Zak, Max, Spike, and Baby Thing,
and little steps that lead to great journeys
—B. M.

For Ethan. Have fun exploring this great world.
—C. L. D.

Margaret K. McElderry Books

An imprint of Simon & Schuster Children's Publishing Division

1230 Avenue of the Americas, New York, New York 10020

Foreword copyright © 2008 by Chris L. Demarest

Illustrations and foreword copyright © 2008 by Bill Mayer

Book design by Ann Bobco

The text for this book is set in Modula Serif.

The illustrations for this book are rendered in airbrush gouache and dyes,

with some digital retouching.

Manufactured in China

10 9 8 7 6 5 4 3 2 1

Library of Congress Cataloging-in-Publication Data

Demarest, Chris L.

All aboard! : a traveling alphabet / concept by Chris L. Demarest ;

illustrated by Bill Mayer.

p. cm.

ISBN-13: 978-0-689-85249-7 (hardcover)

ISBN-10: 0-689-85249-5 (hardcover)

1. Travel—Juvenile literature. 2. Transportation—Juvenile literature.

3. Alphabet books. I. Mayer, Bill. II. Title.

G175.D42 2008

910.4—dc22

2006103006

FIRST EDITION